Dealing With Waste

OLD CLOTHES

Sally Morgan

A+

Smart Apple Media

This book has been published in cooperation with Franklin Watts.

Editor: Rachel Minay, Designer: Brenda Cole, Picture research: Morgan Interactive Ltd., Consultant: Graham Williams

Picture credits
The publishers would like to thank the following for reproducing these photographs:
Alamy 16 (Frank Vetere); Corbis 6 (Jose Luis Pelaez, Inc.), 17 (Musa Farman/EPA); Ecoscene front cover main image (Vicki Coombs), 7 (Chinch Gryniewicz), 8 (Christine Osborne), 9 (Stephen Coyne), 10, 11 (Christine Osborne), 13 (Vicki Coombs), 14, 15, 18 (Ed Maynard), 19 (Eric Needham), 23 (Latha Raman); Imagestate 27 (SO/GRANDEUR NATURE/HOA-QUI); i-stockphoto front cover top right (Vaide Dambrauskaite); Emmeline 4 Re 20 (Mick Eason); Recyclenow.com front cover bottom right; Traid 12 (Darrell Fields), 21 (Vladimir Jansky), 22 (Alessandra Rigillo), 26 (Alastair Guy); Vision Aid Overseas 24 (Brian Donnan), 25 (Paul Constant).

Published in the United States by Smart Apple Media
2140 Howard Drive West, North Mankato, Minnesota 56003

Library of Congress Cataloging-in-Publication Data

Morgan, Sally.
Old clothes / by Sally Morgan.
p. cm. – (Dealing with waste)
Includes index.
ISBN-13: 978-1-59920-011-8
1. Dress accessories–Juvenile literature. 2. Handicraft–Juvenile literature. 3. Recycling (Waste, etc.)–Juvenile literature. I. Title.

TT560.M58 2007
363.72'88–dc22   2006035139

9 8 7 6 5 4 3 2 1

Contents

Throwing away clothes

Everybody needs clothes. As the world's population grows, the demand for clothes increases, and this means that more raw materials are needed to make them.

The racks of clothes in stores often tempt people to buy clothes they don't really need. A surprising number of clothes are never worn.

More clothes

People in developed countries usually have more clothes than those living in developing countries. However, many of the clothes sold in developed countries are made in parts of the world where salaries are lower.

China and Pakistan are among the largest clothes manufacturing countries. Clothes from these countries in the developing world have to be transported thousands of miles to stores in the developed world.

Clothes waste

It is estimated that the average life of a garment in some countries is just three years. Fashion is always changing, so people are always buying new clothes. Also, children grow out of clothes and shoes very quickly. People do not mend or alter clothes as much as they did in the past. Instead, they are thrown away and replaced with new ones. As a result, clothes and shoes make up about 3 percent (by weight) of a typical garbage can in the United States. Most of this is taken with the rest of the garbage to landfill sites, where it is buried.

In this book, you will read about the different types of fibers used to make clothes and how clothes can be reused and recycled.

It's my world!

How far have the clothes in your wardrobe traveled? Look at the labels and see where they were made. Have any been made in your own country? Look at a world map to see how far the clothes have been transported.

In the developing world, it is more common for people to buy fabric and make their own clothes. In this Kenyan market, fabrics are hanging on display.

Materials for clothes

Textile is the name given to any type of material that is made from fibers or threads. There are many different types of textiles. They include woven, knitted, crocheted, and knotted textiles, as well as non-woven ones such as felt.

Plant fibers

Plant fibers that are used to make textiles include cotton and linen. Cotton fiber comes from the fluffy white seed heads of the cotton plant. A plant called flax is used to make linen. Fibers found in the stem of the plant are made into thread and then woven into linen fabric.

Artificial fibers

Over the last 40 years or so, a range of artificial fibers have been used to make clothes. These include nylon, rayon, and polyester. These fibers are made from oil. The artificial fibers can be used on their own to make clothes or mixed with natural fibers. For example, cotton fabric is very comfortable to wear, but it creases easily and needs to be ironed. This can be overcome by weaving polyester into the fabric. Polyester cotton does not crease as much or shrink after washing as much as clothes made from 100% cotton. The different percentages of fibers that the item of clothing is made from is written on the label.

Cotton fibers are found in the seed heads of cotton plants. This cotton farm worker in Turkey is removing the seed heads. In some parts of the world, this is done by machine.

The bark of the rubber tree is cut so that a white liquid called latex oozes out. This is collected and treated to make rubber.

Wool, leather, and rubber

The fleece of animals is made into textiles, too. For example, wool comes from sheep; angora and cashmere come from goats. In addition, there are materials, such as leather and suede, that come from the skin of an animal such as a cow. Rubber for shoe soles is taken from the latex of rubber trees.

It's my world!

Read the labels in your clothes to see which fibers were used to make them. Some fabrics may be a blend of a natural fiber and an artificial one, such as polyester cotton.

Making textiles

All clothes—whether they come from natural or artificial fibers—have an impact on the environment during their manufacture.

Crops and animals

Most farmers spray crops such as cotton and flax with pesticides to kill pests. However, some pesticides may kill useful insects such as bees and ladybugs. Farmers spread fertilizers on the soil to make sure the plants have enough nutrients, and they water the plants during dry weather. Sometimes the fertilizers drain from the soil into rivers, where they cause water pollution.

Sheep, goats, and cattle eat food and produce waste in the form of dung. Also, animals may be sprayed with chemicals to keep flies and other pests away.

Did you know . . .

About 1.1 pounds (0.5 kg) of cotton is needed to make a T-shirt. To obtain this cotton, about 4 ounces (120 g) of pesticides may be used on the cotton plants and 4 gallons (15 l) of water to wash the cotton. A further 46 gallons (175 l) of water may be used in the dyeing process.

Cotton plants are attacked by many pests, such as the cotton bollworm, so the fields have to be sprayed with pesticides many times during the growing season.

From fibers to fabric

The raw materials are taken to factories where they are washed using a lot of water, a valuable but sometimes scarce resource. The cotton or wool is spun to make a yarn. This may be bleached to lose its color, or it may be dyed with chemicals to give it a specific color. These processes create a lot of wastewater. It is too dirty to be allowed to drain into rivers or the sea, so it has to be treated first. The yarn is then transported to factories, where it is woven into different types of fabric. The fabric is then sold to clothing manufacturers who cut it into pieces to make clothes. Then the garments are packaged and transported to shops.

Artificial fibers

Artificial fibers such as nylon and polyester are produced in a factory. This uses electricity and valuable raw materials, such as oil and water. There may be harmful waste products, such as nitrous oxide, from the manufacture of nylon. This gas cannot be allowed to escape into the atmosphere because it contributes to global warming.

Whichever type of fiber a garment is made from, at all stages of its manufacture, energy is used and waste is produced.

The fibers of cotton are taken to a textile factory where they are carded and made into a soft untwisted rope called a sliver, which is spun to make a yarn.

Reduce, reuse, and recycle

To manage waste, we need to reduce, reuse, and recycle. Reduce means to cut down on waste created. Reuse means to put something to a new use. Recycle means to use something again.

Old clothes can be washed and taken to a clothes bank for recycling.

Did you know . . .

More than 70 percent of the world's population regularly wear secondhand clothes.

Reducing clothes waste

Reducing the waste means that clothes manufacturers have to create less waste during the manufacturing process. Sometimes the waste fibers are collected and put back into the yarn-making process. When the fabric is cut up to make up a garment, there are lots of leftover bits. They can be used to make the stuffing for furniture and mattresses.

Reusing clothes

Reusing clothes can mean giving clothes to other people such as family or friends. Alternatively, unwanted clothes can be sold in a secondhand shop, given to a charity, or sold at a garage sale. Charity shops use the money raised from the sale of clothes for good causes. Any clothes that do not sell or are too worn to be reused are recycled instead.

Recycling clothes

Recycling clothes involves reclaiming the fibers from clothes that have no further use and making them into new clothes. Recycling is very efficient because most of a garment can be recycled. Clothes can also be altered or adapted so that they can be used again. Sometimes designer garments and unique accessories are made from recycled fabrics.

Secondhand clothes, books, and household goods can all be sold in charity stores. The money from the sales is for good causes.

Reusing clothes

It is important to try to reuse as many clothes as possible rather than throw them away. Sometimes it is possible to make a simple alteration to get more use out of a garment. Also, clothes can be given to somebody else.

Charity shops

Good-quality clothes can be taken to a charity shop where they can be sold. Shoes, boots, and accessories such as handbags and belts can also all be sold. Most secondhand clothes are sold for between $3 and $20 dollars per item, but some clothes could get $150 or more.

It's my world!

How many clothes in your wardrobe have been given to you by a brother or sister? Have you altered any of the clothes to make them fit?

These racks contain quality secondhand clothes. They have been sorted according to type and size and will be transported to stores, where they will be sold.

These clothes have been collected by clothes banks. Each item will be checked and graded for quality.

Sorting and grading

In most developed countries, there is a network of clothes banks where people can take their unwanted garments, curtains, bed sheets, and shoes. The contents of these clothes banks are taken to sorting centers where experienced workers sort through the clothes. The workers have to identify the type of textile quickly and grade it according to its quality. The best clothes are sent to charity shops. Other wearable clothes are sent overseas. The rest is sent for recycling—about one-fourth of what is collected. The main markets for European secondhand clothes are African countries, Pakistan, and Estonia, Latvia, and Lithuania. The U.S. and Canada often send clothes to South America, Africa, and Pakistan, while Australia and New Zealand usually send clothes to Vietnam, Thailand, and Malaysia.

Clothes aid

After a natural disaster such as an earthquake, volcanic eruption, hurricane, or flood, there is an urgent need for clothes. People who have lost their homes and belongings need emergency supplies of clean clothes, toiletries, and diapers for babies.

Collecting and sorting

Often, emergency clothes collection points are set up where people can take their clothing donations. Then the clothes have to be sorted by volunteers who remove unsuitable or old clothing that nobody would want to wear. Once the clothes have been sorted, they can be shipped by air to the disaster area.

In 2005, Hurricane Katrina devastated New Orleans and the surrounding area in the U.S. Immediately people across the U.S. collected clothes and other items to help those who had been made homeless by the hurricane.

Types of clothes

Clothes are needed in a full range of sizes. Useful items include underwear, shoes, and sensible clothing such as shirts, pants, and sweaters. People usually throw their underwear away rather than recycle it, but secondhand underwear is in great demand after a disaster.

Different climates

Waterproof coats and rubber boots may be needed if it is a wet climate, while blankets, thick coats, scarves, and gloves are needed in mountainous or northern areas where there is cold weather. Clothes for babies and children are also needed.

After the 2005 earthquake in Pakistan, many thousands of people were left homeless. They needed warm winter clothing. This young girl is sitting on a pile of donated clothes.

Did you know ...

On October 8, 2005, a strong earthquake hit the mountainous regions of Pakistan-administered Kashmir and killed 73,000 people. More than 2.5 million people were left homeless. The area has extremely cold winters, so the main priority of the aid organizations was to transport winter tents, blankets, warm clothing, and food into the devastated area before the roads serving the remote villages were cut off by heavy snowfalls.

Recycling clothes

If clothes cannot be reused, then they can be recycled. Recycling clothes is very efficient, and the specialist companies who do this can recycle as much as 95 percent of most clothes, so very little goes to waste.

All of these curtains, sheets, and clothes can be recycled. Sheets can be cut and used as rags, while any towels and blankets may be shredded for stuffing.

Wiping cloths

Almost any fabric can be recycled. Cotton and silk are often used to make rags for a range of industries from cars, to mining, to paper manufacturing. White fabrics are particularly useful. It is far better to recycle fabrics in this way than for people to buy disposable towels, which are used once and thrown away.

Flocking

Garments such as pants and skirts are sold for flocking. The garments are shredded and used as fillers for car insulation, roofing felts, furniture padding, and mattresses. Sometimes the flocking is used as carpet underlay or for soundproofing panels.

Reclaiming fibers

Woolen garments are sent for fiber reclamation. They are sorted according to color, and then the threads are unraveled and made into new clothes. Rags and other items of fabric that are too damaged to be used for clothes or for threads can be shredded and used as shoddy (a woolen fabric made from rags), felt, or padding and stuffing.

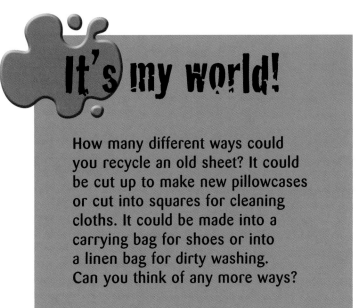

It's my world!

How many different ways could you recycle an old sheet? It could be cut up to make new pillowcases or cut into squares for cleaning cloths. It could be made into a carrying bag for shoes or into a linen bag for dirty washing. Can you think of any more ways?

There are many benefits from recycling clothing. Less waste ends up in landfills, and fewer new clothes are needed, so fewer resources and raw materials are used to make them.

The household waste in this Spanish landfill contains many clothes and old shoes that could have been recycled.

New clothes from old

Some old clothes can be remade into new clothes. There are even specialist companies that make designer clothes from recycled cloth.

Designer clothes

There are clothes designers in many countries who specialize in making desirable designer clothes from quality secondhand clothes. A pair of plain blue jeans, for example, can be transformed into an individual designer item by hand painting designs onto the denim, or a long-sleeved dress can be changed into one with no sleeves. They also use quality secondhand cashmere and angora to make new high-quality sweaters.

An amazing range of clothes and jewelry can be made from the old clothes that are put into clothes recycling banks.

Buttons and bows

Buttons can be removed from old clothes and used on new ones. Decorative bows can be made from strips of colorful material. Strips of fabric can also be made into fabric flowers that could be used to decorate a jacket or suit.

New shoes

There are companies that make shoes from a wide variety of recycled textiles. One company makes shoes from old blankets, leather, men's suits, the silk from parachutes, and towels. The soles are made from recycled rubber.

Unique clothes

A clothes shop has racks of the same style of garment in different sizes and colors. Recycled clothes are different. Every garment is a one-of-a-kind, handmade original, and nobody else will have one exactly the same.

Each item that this model is wearing is unique and has been made from recycled clothes or boots.

Rather than throw clothes away, see if you can alter them so you can wear them again. Try updating an old sweater by adding patchwork from different fabrics. Buttons, bows made from recycled lengths of fabric, or a piece of lace can alter the appearance of a shirt, jacket, or sweater. Fabric bags can be made from an assortment of fabrics. You can get some ideas by visiting some of the Web sites of designers who specialize in making clothes from recycled fabrics.

Developing world

Often people in the developing world cannot afford to buy new clothes, so they have to use secondhand ones. Women are taught to sew, and they can take the cloth from old clothes and make new items out of it.

Shoes and boots

Shoes and boots can be reused or recycled, too. Often, shoes are in good condition, particularly children's shoes, because they grow out of them rather than wear them out. Rubber boots may develop a leak, so they cannot be worn, but the rubber can be recycled.

These old shoes have been taken to a recycling center where they will be sorted according to size. The better-quality shoes will be sold or sent overseas.

Shoe banks

The best way to recycle old shoes and boots is to tie the pairs together and take them to a shoe bank. The shoes are collected and taken to recycling centers.

Sorting and selling

As with clothing, shoes and boots have to be sorted. The good-quality shoes and boots can be sold in charity shops or sent to developing countries where quality shoes are in short supply. For example, good-quality sports shoes are very expensive in Bangladesh, so young people cannot afford to buy them. This means that they have to play in unsuitable footwear that does not protect their feet, such as open-toed sandals.

This man in India is taking apart old shoes so that the valuable parts, such as the rubber sole and the leather, can be reused.

Recycling old shoes

Even very old shoes can be recycled. In many developing countries, the rubber soles from old shoes are removed and stuck on new shoes. Some manufacturers of sports shoes collect old shoes. The rubber soles are removed and ground into granules. The granules can be used to make sports surfaces.

It's my world!

How many pairs of shoes do you own? Do you wear them all? Raw materials and energy are used to make shoes, so make sure you recycle your old shoes so that the materials can be used again.

Old glasses

Millions of people in the developed world wear glasses to correct their sight. However, there are as many as 200 million people in the developing world who see everything through a blurry haze. All they need is a pair of glasses.

This tailor in Burkina Faso needed a pair of glasses so that he could see to carry out his job of making clothes.

Reusing glasses

Just like secondhand clothes, old glasses can be either reused or recycled. There are many opticians and charities that collect old glasses. Any pairs that have broken frames are removed. The quality glasses are then cleaned. They are then sorted according to the strength of the lenses. Any broken frames made of metal can be recycled. The metal is sent to recycling plants, where it will be melted down and reused.

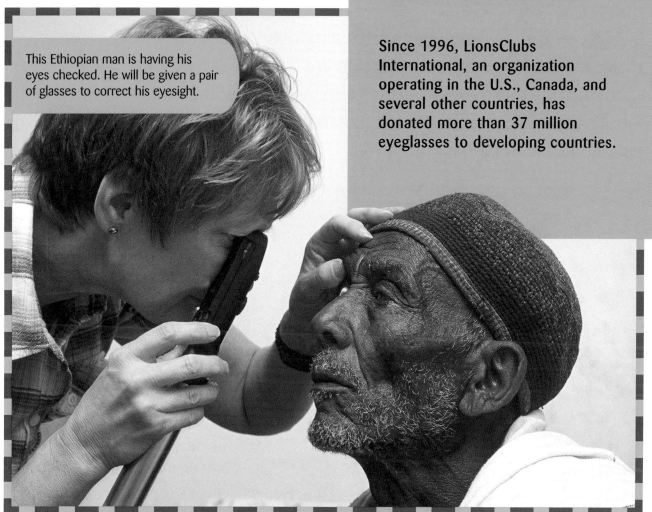

This Ethiopian man is having his eyes checked. He will be given a pair of glasses to correct his eyesight.

It's my world!

Do you or your family have any old pairs of glasses lying in a drawer? You may not be using them because your prescription has changed, but they may be useful to someone living in a developing country. Find out if your local optician collects old glasses.

Restoring eyesight

Secondhand glasses can be shipped to developing countries where they are needed by people with poor eyesight. Some charities send out teams of opticians who train local people to give eye tests. Patients are given a pair of glasses that match their prescription.

The way ahead

Everybody can help reduce the growing quantities of clothes, shoes, and accessories that are thrown away each year. It is also important to think about how the fabrics are made and to reduce the amount of waste created in the manufacturing process.

This model is wearing clothes that have been made from recycled fabrics.

Sustainable fibers

Textiles made from cotton, wool, linen, and other natural fibers are described as sustainable. This is because the crops can be replanted or more animals bred so there is a continuous supply of the raw materials into the future. Textiles made from rayon or polyester come from oil, which is an unsustainable raw material. Fossil fuels such as oil, gas, and coal are being used up at a far more rapid rate than they are being made, so the supply will run out. Scientists estimate that there is only a 30- to 50-year supply of oil left. By choosing natural fibers, you can help reduce the use of fossil fuels.

Environmentally friendly fibers

Organic cotton is grown without the use of pesticides and chemical fertilizers. The yields are lower, but there is less damage to the environment because unbleached cotton fibers are not treated with chemicals and less waste water is produced when it is manufactured.

Hemp—the way forward

Hemp is a very useful crop that can be used as a fuel and to make paper, plastics, and fabrics. Until the 1820s, it was used to make about 80 percent of the textiles in Europe and North America. It was also the main oil used in lights before the arrival of electricity. Slowly, its use declined as it was replaced by cotton and oil. However, it is being rediscovered, and the amount of hemp grown in the world is increasing once again. This crop could be grown to provide a sustainable source of oil and fibers.

Hemp grows to about 6.5 feet (2 m) in height and the long fibers, shown here, come from the stem. Steam is used to separate the fibers from the stem.

It's my world!

What can you do?

▸ Think before you buy new clothes—do you need to buy something, or can you use what you already have in your wardrobe?

▸ Update your clothes by adding buttons, lace, patches, or fabric paint to give them a fresh look.

▸ Buy clothes from secondhand or charity shops. You can save money, help the environment, and support a charity at the same time.

▸ Never throw textiles in the trash, even small items, because they can all be recycled. Wash the textiles and take them to the nearest clothes bank.

▸ Recycle shoes and boots, too.

▸ Take old glasses to an optician so they can be reused or recycled.

Glossary

Developed country
a country in which most people have a high standard of living

Developing country
a country in which most people have a low standard of living and less access to goods and services compared to people in a developed country

Fertilizer
a source of nutrients sprayed onto soil to supply plants with all their requirements for growth

Flocking
shredded textiles used for padding or filling

Fossil fuel
a fuel formed over millions of years from the remains of plants and animals, for example; peat, coal, crude oil, and natural gas

Landfill
a large hole in the ground used to dispose of waste

Pesticide
a chemical that is used to kill pests

Recycle
to process and reuse materials in order to make new items

Reduce
to lower the amount of waste that is produced

Reuse
to use something again, either in the same way or in a different way

Sustainable
describes a resource that will not run out or can continue to be manufactured in the future without harming the environment

Textile
a material made from fibers or threads

Unsustainable
describes a level of use of a resource that cannot be maintained in the future, which will cause the resource to run out

Waste
anything that is thrown away, abandoned, or released into the environment in a way that could harm the environment

Yarn
spun fibers or thread, used in the production of textiles

Web sites

Earth 911

www.earth011.org/master.asp

This Web site shows a variety of national and local U.S. recycling programs and events.

Lions Recycle for Sight

www.lionsclubs.org/EN/cntent/vision_eyeglass_sight.shtml

This Web site provides lists of recycling centers and a video about the recycling journey of a pair of eyeglasses.

Recycling and Waste Prevention

www.metro_region.org/article.cfm?articleid=16738

This Web site provides links to other sites about textile recycling.

Tokyo Recycle Project

www.powerhousemuseum.com/tokyorecycle/

An exhibition that is being shown around the world on the work of Masahiro Nakagawa, designer of the popular Japanese streetwear label 20471120. Instead of creating new garments from scratch, Nakagawa and his team of recyclers breathe new life into old and worn garments.

U.S. Environmental Protection Agency

www.epa.gov

This Web site has lots of environmental information on all issues, not just waste.

U.S. Recycling

www.usrecycleink.com

At this site, learn about recycling fundraisers.

Index